A CHECK UP FROM THE NECK UP

LEARN EXACTLY WHAT IS NECESSARY FOR YOUR FUTURE

DALE CARNEGIE BRONNER

A Check Up From The Neck Up, Learn exactly what is necessary for your future.
By Dale Carnegie Bronner
Published by Carnegie Books
212 Riverside Pkwy
Austell, GA 30168
www.DALEBRONNER.com

ISBN 978-0-9891356-0-3

Contents

✓ ARE YOU READY FOR YOUR CHECKUP?

What do you think the doctor would say if, during your annual medical exam, you refused to cooperate?

"Stick out your tongue and say, Aah!" says the physician.

"No," you reply," I don't feel like doing that!"

"Well, let me check your blood pressure," he continues.

"Don't bother," you insist. "I had that done last year and it was fine."

It wouldn't take long before the doctor would escort you out of his office and quietly remove your name from his patient roster.

If you plan to live a healthy, productive life, the decision to have periodic thorough checkups must be *yours*!

A FULL INSPECTION

On the pages that follow you will be given a self-examination that involves your thinking, your speech, your vision, your decision making, and much more. I call it "A Checkup from the

Neck Up!"

However, these seeds will not take root unless you make a personal choice to receive them. Like the psalmist, you must say *"Examine me, O Lord, and prove me; try my mind and my heart"* (Psalm 26:2 NKJV).

If you want to know what God has in store for your life, ask Him for an in-depth examination and look forward to hearing the results. To make sure you are on the right track in life, a good question to ask yourself is, "How do I want to be remembered?"

- Nehemiah was just a doorkeeper in the house of the king, yet the Lord saw his potential and asked him to rebuild the walls of Jerusalem.
- Joseph was exiled from Israel, but he had a mind and heart for God and was elevated to reign with the governor of Egypt.
- David was only a shepherd boy when the Lord examined his life and declared, *"I have found David the son of Jesse, a man after mine own heart, which shall fulfil all my will"* (Acts 13:22)

HARD LESSONS

Never forget that King David trained before he reigned.

He was anointed with oil that ran down his head, however, for the next fifteen years he had to run for his life. There were twenty-one attempts made to kill him.

It is more than one step from a sheep pasture to the king's palace. There were many tests along the way.

In the early church, Saul was a tormentor of Christians before his Damascus Road experience. At that moment the Lord transformed his life and gave him a new name – Paul.

Some people think he immediately set off for his great missionary journeys. No. For three years, Paul studied in the city of Petra. God put him in a rigorous school in the "City of the Rock." That's where he learned the lessons needed to evangelize the known world and write two-thirds of the New Testament. Because of what Paul experienced, he could tell the believers at Corinth, *"Examine yourselves, whether ye be in the faith; prove your own selves"* (2 Corinthians 13:5).

ARE YOU PREPARED?

We may wonder, "Why did God send me to this city?" Or, "Why did the Lord permit this person to come into my life?" I believe the Father allows what we see and hear to prepare us for service – for the equipping of the saints (Ephesians 4:12). The Lord will call you, prepare you, then He will commission you.

Don't confuse your call with your commission. There is a strenuous training and examination period in between.

Heaven's X-ray machine sees everything! God knows exactly what is necessary for your future.

Have you ever opened a gift box at Christmas and noticed the words "Assembly Required"? That's exactly how it is when we first come to Christ. There are pieces of our heart, spirit and mind that must be properly joined together. We cannot be used to our peak potential until we are fully assembled.

A NEW VIEW

In addition to the Lord watching our lives, He asks us to take an introspective look at ourselves. Before partaking of communion, we are given this warning: *"But let a man examine himself, and so let him eat of that bread, and drink of that cup"* (1 Corinthians 11:28).

The price of ignorance is steep. *"For he who eats and drinks is an unworthy manner eats and drinks judgment to himself, not discerning the Lord's body. For this reason many are weak and sick among you, and many sleep"* (vv.29-30 NKJV).

- I believe you are ready for that examination.
- In these chapters you will be asked:
- What are the strongholds of your life?
- Can you define your core beliefs?
- What thoughts dominate your mind?
- What is the impact of your words?
- How does your will line up with God's?
- What is the key to successful decision making?
- How is your vision?
- Are the weapons you use carnal or spiritual?

It is my prayer that the Lord will allow you to see yourself in a new light – that He will stretch your vision and take you to a higher level of excellence.

1

✓ CHECK YOUR STRONGHOLDS

A gentleman approached me after a service and confessed, "Pastor, I've been prayed for, anointed with oil, and had the devil cast out of me. Still, there are certain things that won't leave my life."

It was obvious to me the man had a stronghold – something that had a strong hold on his life. "Sir," I told him, "Perhaps it is time to deal with the problem yourself!" God wants you to personally take charge of the situation!"

You too may be struggling with a similar dilemma and ask, "Can't I just bind this thing?"

It is true that Jesus declared, *"Whatsoever ye shall bind on earth shall be bound in heaven: and whatsoever ye shall loose on earth shall be loosed in heaven"* (Matthew 18:18).

However, we cannot use this principle to deal with strongholds. There are more issues involved. For example, when

David killed Goliath, he did not realize the giant had four other brothers, and it took him forty years to destroy them.

A LARGER PROBLEM

Perhaps you have heard the expression, "When you lay down with dogs, you get up with fleas." Just because you separate yourself from the dog, doesn't mean you are free of fleas.

You can't simply say, "I bind this stronghold," since you are most likely still a carrier of this problem.

I remember the time when a winter storm uprooted a dogwood tree in our backyard. It toppled over and I thought, "I'll wait until the weather warms up before I remove it."

When spring arrived, I could hardly believe my eyes. That fallen tree began to bloom! The buds popped out and produced a beautiful display of color. You see, the tree had fallen, but some roots were still connected!

You may tackle one specific thing, but have you addressed the entire issue?

In Scripture, there is no account of Jesus ever binding an evil spirit or demon. He either rebuked them, or told them to leave. Shackling what is evil will simply restraint or deactivate a spirit's power; it is not a total resolution to the problem.

WHERE DOES IT BEGIN?

You may ask, "What actually is a stronghold? How is it defined?"

A stronghold is a fortress of wrongful thoughts that are formed in your mind and affect your life.

It gives the enemy a protected place of influence.

Let me reiterate, strongholds are not in heaven; they are in your mind, and must be pulled down.

Every temptation is first presented to your thought life. Eve looked at the tree and saw that "it was good." Mentally, she was attracted to something that distracted her away from God's will.

I've met people who believe that spiritual welfare is about reaching into the air and rebuking the spirits of Satan. No. You don't have to climb a mountain or reach the 30th floor of a skyscraper to engage in a skirmish with Satan.

The battle is fought between your ears!

Your mind is the high place where the conflict is raging.

TAKING ROOT!

A stronghold over your life is established by a progression of events. Let me give you an example. Perhaps a friend offers you a taste of nicotine to sooth your nerves. Soon you may have a craving for other "ines" – caffeine or even cocaine.

In other cases, something unusual transpires that triggers an opening for a stronghold to take root.

Here is the process:

1. A traumatic experience produces wrong patterns of thinking.

2. Wrong patterns of thinking produces wrong behavior.
3. Wrong behavior helps erect a stronghold to protect your right to do as you please. It says, "Well, if this is the way I want to live my life, I ought to be able to."
4. This perpetuates the pain by keeping the trauma locked in – and God locked out.

INTO CAPTIVITY

How are we to remove Satan's hold over our life? Scripture makes it clear. Paul wrote, *"For though we walk in the flesh, we do not war after the flesh (For the weapons of our welfare are not carnal, but might through God to the pulling down of strong holds): Casting down imaginations, and every high thing that exalteth itself against the knowledge of God, and bringing into captivity every thought to the obedience of Christ; And having a readiness to revenge all disobedience, when your obedience is fulfilled"* (2 Corinthians 10:3-6).

There is a war in progress and you need to be prepared. A vital part of the armor of God is *"the helmet of salvation"* (Ephesians 6:17). He places something over your heard to guard and preserve your mind.

Your spirit may be born again, but your thoughts must be constantly refreshed. Paul tells us to *"be renewed in the spirit of your mind"* (Ephesians 4:23).

REPLACE IT!

To successfully deal with strongholds, you must demolish the old and replace it with something new.

It is not enough to go to Alcoholics Anonymous and declare you will not drink. You must find a replacement. It is also true with drugs. The same evil that first influenced you will attempt to re-inhabit you again unless you replace the habit with behavior that is positive.

Every empty space is going to be filled with *something*. The Bible says, *"Neither give place to the devil"* (Ephesians 4:27). If you give Satan an inch, he will take a yard! Don't allow him access.

You cannot control what thoughts come to you, but you have the power to determine which ones *stay*.

Tell yourself, "I am not going to think this way because that train of thought is headed for the wrong destination"

The Word tells us, *"And be not conformed to this world" but be ye transformed by the renewing of your mind"* (Romans 12:2).

THE DECEIVER

By attacking our mind, Satan locks us into addictive and habitual behavior. That's how he holds God's people hostage. I have met saved, sanctified, Bible totin', scripture quotin' believers who are still dealing with strongholds. They don't like to admit the fact they are struggling with situations beyond their control.

Every fortress of Satan is set up through deception. Scripture declares the master deceiver *'was a murderer from the beginning, and abode not in the truth, because there is no truth in him. When he speaketh a lie, he speaketh of his own: for he is a liar and the father of it"* (John 8:44).

To many, his falsehoods are accepted and believed. They become truth, giving the devil a protected place of influence.

When a concerned mother says, "Honey, I have been there. You are making the wrong decision," the devil confuses your mind with lies.

"You don't need to listen to her." he chides. "She just doesn't want you to have any fun!"

Satan is sly. For example, the initial reaction to drugs is usually positive – otherwise he couldn't entice people to try. The liabilities come later.

IT'S A SYSTEM

This may come as a shock to you, but Satan does not have real power – he only has influence.

Instead of physically controlling you, the devil preys on your weakness.

He induces you to take the path of least resistance.

The man and woman who become entangled in an illicit sexual relationship are not forced into the trap; they are enticed by Satan.

The devil doesn't need to enter your being and tell you what to do. Instead, he sets up a hold over you – which is systemic in nature. It is a system that becomes so entrenched that it will continue to function long after you have cast him out.

Are you beginning to see why a stronghold is not easily confronted? You have to change the entire process, which does not happen overnight.

EXCUSES! EXCUSES!

Here are five great hindrances to our lives:

1. **Fear** – worry and anxiety can paralyze your progress.
2. **Unrecognized resources** – help is available if we will only open our eyes
3. **Comfort zone mentality** – we close the door to our future by being too easily satisfied.
4. **An inferiority complex** – we must see ourselves as children of the King, worthy of His best.
5. **Excuses** – finding reasons for failure.

If you are serious about removing the holds on your life, start disposing of the excuses that keep you trapped where you are.

You can always find an alibi for inaction:

- "I don't want to go jogging because I might be hit by a car!"
- "What's the point of buying stock? The market may crash!"
- "Why do I need to go to church? I can watch the preacher on television."

Millions find a cop-out for failure by blaming their environment, their upbringing, "the system", their age, their sex, their race or lack of finances.

If you look for an excuse, you will always find one – without exception.

TROUBLED WATERS

A man who had been lame for 38 years sat at the pool of Bethesda, waiting for the waters to be troubled. In those days, *"an angel went down at a certain time into the pool and stirred up the water; then whoever stepped in first, after the stirring of the water, was made well of whatever disease he had"* (John 5:4 NKJV).

Jesus saw the man lying there and knew he had been in that condition a long time. He said to him, *"Do you want to be made well?"* (v.6).

The sick man answered Him, *"Sir, I have no man to put me into the pool when the water is stirred up; but while I am coming, another steps down before me"* (v.7).

Excuses had prolonged the man's infirmity.

He must have been surprised when Jesus declared, *"Rise, take up your bed and walk"* (v.8). Immediately, the man was healed.

YOUR GREAT FUTURE

Ask yourself, "What excuse is holding me back?"

If you need to be on a diet, don't tell people, "My family is just big-boned!" That's a weak justification.

Excuses are crutches for the uncommitted.

Break free! Eliminate the ties that keep you bound.

Clear your mind of everything that restricts your growth.

Stop telling yourself, "This is all I can handle!" Who told you that ?

If you will increase the size of your container, the Lord will cause your roots to expand. God grows things according to the size of the vessel.

How do you expect to change if you allow yourself to blame your present circumstances? Stop saying, "If I only had a chance or an opportunity." *We all have opportunities every day!*

Don't dwell on the mistakes of yesterday. You can't erase where you have been, but you can certainly change where you are going. Remember, every saint has a past, and every sinner has a future.

I had absolutely no control over the circumstances under which I was born, yet I certainly have something to do with the way I will *finish* my life.

TRAPPED IN A WEB

Many attempt to change their behavior without trying to correct the stronghold. That never works!

It's like reaching up and removing a spider web with a broom. It's a temporary solution. You also have to remove the spider – the culprit that keeps spinning the webs.

No matter where you live, there are spiders – in the homes of both the poor and the rich. The Bible says, *"The spider skillfully grasps with its hands, and it is in kings' palaces"* (Proverbs 30:28 NKJV).

It is not an accident the Internet is called the "world wide web." It has snared millions into pornography, gambling and other obsessions.

Start dealing with the spider!

WHAT MAKES US AFRAID?

Fear is a major stronghold.

We are the sum total of everything that has been spoken into our lives. That is what produces our feelings, insecurities, anxieties and phobias.

The average man has at least two phobias in his life – and the average woman has nearly four. Here are just a few:

- Aerophobia – the fear of heights
- Aviophobia – the fear of flying
- Ophidiophobia – the fear of snakes
- Pryophobia – the fear of fire.
- Triskadekaphobia – the fear of number 13.

Usually, high rise buildings don't have a number thirteen button in the elevators. It makes people feel better to press "14" – even if it is actually the thirteenth floor.

We need to realize that there is a difference between the emotion of fear and the *spirit* of fear.

- The emotion of fear is God-given and helps to protect us.
- The spirit of fear puts us in bondage.

It is totally natural to stand before an audience and be a little nervous. Emotionally, you say, "Lord, I am frightened. I am trusting you to help me."

You are not acting in the absence of anxiety, but in the presence of fear – trusting and trembling. Eventually, you will triumph.

The spirit of fear, however, does not come from the Father. The Apostle Paul declared, *"For God hath not given us a spirit of fear; but of power, and of love, and of a sound mind"* (2 Timothy 1:7).

"WHY AM I FRIGHTENED?"

A 73-year old woman from Detroit traveled to Africa for the express purpose of having me pray for her.

I tried to arrange a meeting at my office, but she was so consumed with tension and anxiety she was too frightened to leave her hotel room.

The woman was bound by a stronghold of fear!

I learned that she had not left her home for several months before making the trip to meet me.

We went to the hotel and I began to share what God's Word says concerning faith and that *"perfect love casts out fear"* (1 John 4:18 NKJV).

After discussing many scriptures on the topic and praying with her, I turned to walk out the door. She stopped me with these words: "Pastor, why do I still feel so scared?"

With my hand on the door knob, I replied, "I really don't know."

At that instant the Spirit of the Lord came upon me. My body turned toward her and my hand reached out. She bent over and began to scream. Immediately, every demon of fear that had dominated her life departed. What a glorious time of deliverance that was!

The woman returned to Detroit and I heard from her several months later. She was rejoicing and exclaimed, "I have been out of the house every day and am once again running my business."

God not only restored her life, He permanently removed her fear.

TAKE CONTROL

Some people pray, "Please, Lord. Tear down this stronghold!" Those words aren't always necessary. Why? Because you have been placed in the custodial care of your temple by the Father.

God says, "I have already given you the power. Why are you waiting?"

You can remove Satan's grip on your life by making not only *right* decisions, but *righteous* decisions.

With every spiritual choice we make, a hold on our life is systematically torn down. And once it is destroyed, fill the void with something beautiful, something good – something from God.

Dr. Bronner's Checklist:

- ✓ Recognize that strongholds reside in your mind.
- ✓ Beware of wrong thinking that produces wrong behavior.
- ✓ Protect yourself with the helmet of salvation
- ✓ Replace a negative habit with something positive.
- ✓ Eliminate your excuses for failure.

✓ Ask God to remove the spirit of fear.

There is only one place a stronghold belongs: under your feet! According to the Word, *"...the Lord will make you the head and not the tail; you shall be above only, and not be beneath"* (Deuteronomy 28:13 NKJV).

Declare victory today!

2

✓ CHECK YOUR CORE BELIEFS

A primary reason we need a checkup from the neck up is that *faulty thinking and false information produces wrong beliefs.*

As time passes, these beliefs result in flawed thinking and we are trapped in a vicious cycle.

For example, some people are raised with a do-your-own-thing philosophy: "Don't ever depend on anybody. You need to take care of yourself."

When they repeat their wedding vows, however, they are suddenly faced with the principle of being submitted one to another – and the concept is foreign.

For a marriage to work both parties must discard their independent attitudes.

One man told me, "I was taught to believe that there are no

absolutes. Then, when I began to study God's Word, I realized I was wrong."

The Bible leaves no "wiggle room" regarding right and wrong, sin and salvation. God says, *"Woe unto them that call evil good, and good evil"* (Isaiah 5:20). The Almighty declares, *"For I am the Lord, I change not"* (Malachi 3:6).

Satan will exploit your wrong opinions to keep you from God's blessing.

WHAT CONTROLS YOUR ACTIONS?

Belief is the mental acceptance of something that appears to be deserving of confidence and trust. It is a system that drives your behavior. It is not a matter of, "Are my parents watching me?" "Is my spouse around?"

It does not matter who is with you, rather what is in you.

That's what controls you actions. Remember this: You are going to be who you are regardless of where you are.

You may encounter great ideas, excellent teaching, even truth. Yet if these are not accepted in your core belief system, you won't act upon them.

Just because you confront someone with negative truth doesn't mean the issue is settled. The individual must believe it before change can occur.

This will not happen unless they become fully convinced that what they are doing – or how they are doing it – is wrong.

A LESSON FROM NAZARETH

The reputation of Jesus as a miracle-worker spread throughout the land, yet when He came to His hometown there was unbelief – and the miracles practically ceased.

Scripture records that when He taught at the synagogue in Nazareth, the people questioned, *"Is this not the carpenter, the Son of Mary, and brother of James, Joses, Judas, and Simon? And are not His sisters here with us?"* (Mark 6:3 NKJV). They took offense at Him.

They said, "He is just one of us. We know the family."

Familiarity was about to rob them of being able to receive miraculous blessings from His hands.

Jesus replied, *"A prophet is not without honor except in his own country, among his own relatives, and in his own house"* (v.4).

THE COST OF DOUBT

What was the result of their negative thinking? The Bible says, *"He could do no mighty work there, except that He laid His hands on a few sick people and healed them. And He marveled because of their unbelief"* (vv.5-6).

There were no blind eyes opened or deaf ears unstopped, only minor healings. Why? He was in an atmosphere of skepticism!

What did Jesus do about the situation? He addressed the issue of their core beliefs. The Bible says, *"He went about the villages in a circuit, teaching"* (v.6).

Jesus not only preached, He taught and explained the Good News. He caused them to see and understand – and He made the Gospel relevant to their culture.

TEACHING PRECEDES MIRACLES

A short while later, a large crowd – about five thousand – gathered around Jesus and the disciples in the wilderness. The Lord *'was moved with compassion toward them, because they were as sheep not having a shepherd: and he began to teach them many things"* (Mark 6:34).

Again, instruction was at the heart of His ministry.

The large event lasted several days and the disciples because concerned. "These people don't have anything to eat," they told the Lord. And the multitude was too weak to walk back home Jesus responded, "How many loaves do you have?" The disciples answered, "Five, and two fishes" (v.38).

Jesus *"looked up to heaven, and blessed, and broke the loaves, and gave them to his disciples to set before them; and the two fishes divided he among them all"*

What a miracle! The loaves and fishes multiplied and every person was fed. It was a demonstration of what Christ was teaching. God confirmed His Word with signs following.

YOU'LL KNOW IT!

Jesus said, *"And ye shall know the truth, and the truth shall make you free"* (John 8:32). It will restore you to God's original purpose for your life.

When God speaks divinely and prophetically to you, the words will resonate throughout your entire being. You will know it is the Lord speaking – and you will believe !

You won't hear His voice just once; it will come again and again. And when that call is clear, you – and everyone around you – will know it. You may even travel to another city and a total stranger will say, "I've never met you, but I believe you have the call of God on your life."

A PRECIOUS NAME

I am extremely protective about what I believe – which means I am protective of Jesus.

Please know that I am not a violent person, but something on the inside of me rises up when I hear someone take the Lords name in vain. I can hardly tolerate it!

That name is precious to me, for it is Jesus who transformed my life and set me free. And when I pray in His name, I see His wonder-working power.

The name of Jesus is not simply a word, He is at the very center of my being.

FALSELY ACCUSED

I love the story of Joseph.

After he was sold into Egyptian slavery by his brothers, he was working in the house of Potiphar – the captain of Pharaoh's guards.

Perhaps you have read the account of how Potiphar's wife desired to be intimate with Joseph in a manner that was inappropriate and adulterous.

On one occasion, *"when Joseph went into the house to do his work, and none of the men of the house was inside...she caught him by garment, saying, "Lie with me.' But he left his garment in her hand, and fled and ran outside"* (Genesis 39:11-12 NKJV).

Why did Joseph flee? He immediately relied on his core belief and said, "I fear God too much." That is what controlled his behavior.

He did not say, "No, I respect Mr. Potiphar too much." Instead he turned to his reliance on God and thought, "I don't want to ruin my relationship with the Lord!" He wasn't about to mortgage his future by an act of sin.

After Joseph was falsely accused and thrown in prison, he had so much favor with the jailer that he was placed in charge – and eventually was named a governor in Egypt!

God saw Joseph's great belief and rewarded him with a royal promotion.

MAKE IT A HABIT

You will never alter your behavior just because you heard a good idea and decided to try it. Research shows that it takes at least twenty-one days of repetition to form a habit. Don't weaken and give up after three days or even one week!

You need to repeat the same activity – in the exact same way

for twenty – one days!

Prior to Daniel receiving his great vision from God, he prayed for *"three full weeks"* (Daniel 10:2 NLJV). As the prophet writes, *"I ate no pleasant food, no meat or win came into my mouth, nor did I anoint myself at all, till three whole weeks were fulfilled"* (v.3).

Before the answer arrived, Daniel developed a habit of prayer.

A WORD FROM GOD

Some individuals get excited about a message on Sunday morning and say, "Thank You, Lord. That was a word especially for me!"

The next week, if you ask what God told them, they don't have the foggiest notion. "It was a good message, but I can't exactly remember what the preacher said."

Let me suggest that when God gives you a word, get the tape and play it in your car for the next twenty-one days. Every day!

"WRITE THE VISION"

I remember observing a woman who had just received a prophecy from the Lord. She was exuberant; shouting and crying so much I wondered if she truly heard what was being said!

When you receive a word of prophecy, write it down. Place it in your Bible or on a mirror so you will see it again and again.

Repeat it in your mind.

it plain upon tables, that he may run that readeth it"

(Habakkuk 2:2).

Speak the prophecy out loud and rekindle the fire. Why? If you don't say faithful to God's vision people may start talking you out of it. That's why we need to constantly be refueled, refocused and restored to the message of the Lord.

Act on your vision!

I smile when I visit homes and see exercise equipment collecting dust in the corner – stationary bicycles, row machines, treadmills, and even ab-busters!

"It seemed like a good idea at the time," one owner embarrassingly confided. Obviously, it is a lot easier to make a habit of eating fried chicken and mashed potatoes!

START EARLY

Whoever has the first chance to teach a child creates strongholds in his or her life – whether the information is true or false.

I learned many years ago that every lie that is believed becomes truth.

It is imperative that children receive the teaching of God's Word from the time they are able to comprehend.

Stories from the Bible should be read at bedtime, and children need to memorize important verses so they can quote them.

What is in their mind and heart will become a spiritual shield for a lifetime. Later, when someone tries to question their faith or introduce a false dogma, an alarm will sound. Their mind and heart won't blindly receive it.

Every mom and dad needs to build that hedge of protection for their child.

A LIFE-GIVING FORCE

I have always considered myself to be an average person with an above-average God – just an ordinary man with an extraordinary faith.

The Gospel of Christ has changed my life because I stayed in the Word – day after day, night after night.

I made a habit of saturating my life with Scripture. It transformed my thinking, fortified my faith, and Established my beliefs.

Jesus declared to those who believed on Him, *"If ye continue in my word, then are ye my disciples indeed"* (John 8:31).

What flows from my lips is a direct reflection of what He has firmly placed within me. It is a life-giving force.

From personal experience I can tell you that what Jesus said is true: *"He that believeth on me, as the scripture hath said, out of his belly shall flow rivers of living water"* (John 7:38).

What enters your mind finds its way to your heart – then it

is expressed in your words and actions. The Bible tells us, *"For as he thinketh in his heart, so he is"* (Proverbs 23:7). And *"out of the abundance of the heart the mouth speaketh"* (Matthew 12:34).

Immerse yourself in the Word.

There are times when something begins to well up inside me and I boldly say, "I can do all things through Christ who strengthens me."

Those words did not originate with me, and certainly are not a statement of conceit or arrogance. It is a confidence I have in God and His divine Word.

When the Lord is in the foundation of your faith and belief nothing will seem impossible.

Dr. Bronner's Checklist:

✓ Faulty thinking produces wrong beliefs.
✓ Your belief system drives your behavior.
✓ Miracles are hindered because of doubt.
✓ To form a habit, repeat the behavior for at least twenty-one days.
✓ Every lie that is accepted becomes truth.
✓ What enters your mind finds its way to your heart.

Dr. Martin Luther King said, "If a man is not willing to die for what he believes that man is not fit to live."

Today, take an inventory of your core beliefs.

3

✓ CHECK YOUR CORE BELIEFS

I don't claim to understand everything that goes on in our world, yet some questions make me smile:

- Why do we park on a driveway and drive on a parkway?
- When traffic moves the slowest, why is it called "rush hour"?
- Why don't we ever read a headline that says, "Psychic Wins Lottery"?
- When women wear lipstick, why do their lips still move?
- Why do we entrust our money to people called "brokers"?

While I am not sure about the answers, at least the questions prod my thinking – which is an activity far few people engage in these days.

IN A DAZE!

Have you ever found yourself driving home and your mind drifts into the twilight zone? The radio is playing, you are talking on the cell phone and the next thing you know you are pulling into your driveway, and don't even remember getting there!

You were on autopilot – guided home by your subconscious because it knows the way.

The next morning you go through the routine of brushing your teeth and combing your hair – almost in a daze. We have repeated the drill so many times it is automatic.

"MUSCLE MEMORY"

It is estimated that 95 percent of our decisions are made from the subconscious. The activity is programmed into our muscle memory. That's how we do everything, from roller skating to knitting.

The reason we don't think about breathing is because it is involuntary. Our body knows how to respond.

When the things of God permeate our lives, we will react to situations without struggle. Even in an emergency, faith will begin to flow.

Instinctively, you will declare, "The joy of the Lord is my strength!"

In the midst of a tragedy you will find yourself saying, "God you will have all things in control."

CLEAN YOUR ENGINE!

Our mind is an amazing instrument. What you put into your brain affects more than your thinking. It makes a tremendous impact on what you see and hear.

You recognize images because of the optic nerve that runs to your brain. You also have an auditory nerve connected to your mind that instantly translated the sounds you heart.

Without thousands of connections working harmoniously together we could not function. And if we don't clean the parts periodically, we become like an engine without an oil change – all clogged up.

AMUSEMENT?

More than once our entire family has gone on a one-week television fast. It makes you realize how much power the media has over your life.

Most of the time, television is nothing more than mind-numbing amusement. The word amuse gives you an indication of what is involved. If you break the word apart, the first letter "a" is the Latin prefix that indicates *none or not.* And *must* means *thinking*. Therefore, "amuse" can be defined as *not thinking*!

The next time you are watching your favorite program contemplate the word. Television is doing your thinking for you!

A GOOD IDEA?

Beware of wrong mind-patterns – they can produce wrong action.

Unless the Lord clearly directs you, be cautious. What might be a God idea for one person may only be a *good idea* for another.

Don't assume that because a friend makes a suggestion, it is automatically right for you. Perhaps it works in their life, yet in yours, the key may unlock the wrong door.

In my younger days I had a friend who suffered a mental breakdown over the paranoia that people were talking about him.

Even worse, he told me, "People are talking about *us*!"

THE "PAIN MAKER!"

If your current mental system has negatively affected your life, it's time to change your way of thinking.

How would you feel if you had been named "Sorry" – and your mother referred to you as a "pain maker"? That is exactly what happened to Jabez, a man we read about in the Old Testament. The Bible records that "his mother called his name Jabez, saying, Because I bare him with sorry" (1 Chronicles 4:9).

Every time someone spoke his name, Jabez was reminded that he was "the one who causes pain," or a "sorry person." I can only imagine what an indelible mark was etched on his mind.

What a mistake! Whether out of ignorance or intention, his mother gave him a name based on what was - not on what should have been.

"CHANGE MY THINKING"

In desperation, Jabez cried out to the God of Israel, *"Oh that thou wouldest bless me indeed, and enlarge my coast, and that thine hand might be with me, and that thou wouldest keep me from evil, that it may not grieve me!"* (v.10).

He was saying, "All my life I have done nothing but cause trouble – and have disappointed everyone in my family. I need to be blessed. Change my thinking and enlarge my borders. Let Your hand be with me."

What was the result of that prayer? The Bible says, *"And God granted him that which he requested"* (v.10).

You may be surprised at the results if you just ask for the Lord's help. If you don't like your life story, rewrite it !

That's what Jabez did. Before Jabez asked God to bless him, the preceding verse points out that *"Jabez was more honorable than his brothers."* When you are honorable, you can ask God for anything! Despite his name, the thoughts of Jabez made him honorable.

Regardless of your upbringing, when you turn to the Almighty everything changes – your thoughts, your attitude and your future. Paul wrote, *"Brethren, be not children in understanding... but in understanding be men"* (1 Corinthians 14:20).

TALK TO YOURSELF?

To fill your mind and spirit with the things of God you need to meditate. The Hebrew word of hagah – which translated means to ponder, imagine, to study or speak to oneself.

Paul told the believers at Ephesus, *"And be not drunk with wine, wherein is excess; but be filled with the Spirit; speaking to yourselves in psalms and hymns and spiritual songs, singing and making melody in your heart to the Lord"* (Ephesians 5:18-19). You may be considered crazy for talking to yourself, yet as you can see, it is scriptural. You can call "those things which be not as though they were" (Romans 4:17).

Go ahead! Speak God's best into your thoughts Over and over again. Say to yourself, "My child is healed!" "That is my house!"

TIME TO MEDITATE

Don't be apprehensive of the word meditation. We sometimes avoid the concept because of its association with Eastern practices of tantra, yoga and transcendental meditation.

What I am referring to is based on the Word. Scripture tells us, *"This book of the law shall not depart out of thy mouth; but thou shalt meditate therein day and night, that thou mayest observe to do according to all that is written therein: for then thou shalt make thy way prosperous, and then thou shalt have good success"* (Joshua 1:8).

The Bible does not say that God is going to universally give success to all His children – only those who follow His ways: It's up to you!

- ...out of your mouth.
- ...you shall meditate therein.
- ...that you may observe and do.
- ...then you shall make your way prosperous.

- ...then you shall have good success.

We have the power to control our activities and thoughts. For example, regardless of the struggles you face at work, you should make a conscious effort not to bring your war-stories home. When you leave your place of employment, close the door and tell yourself, "I am not going to deal with this until I return tomorrow."

FOCUS YOUR FAITH

To some New Age practitioners, meditation involves clearing your mind or "blanking out." To a Christian, it is just the opposite; your mind becomes intense on an area where you choose the focus of your faith.

For example, if you are physically sick you need to dwell on a particular verse from the Word: *"If you diligently heed the voice of the Lord your God and do what is right in His sight, give ear to His commandments and keep all His statues, I will put none of the diseases on you which I have brought on the Egyptians. For I am the Lord who heals you"* (Exodus 15:26 NKJV).

A SURE-FIRE RECIPE

The Word tells us specifically what to think about – and it is all positive: *"Finally, brethren, whatsoever things are true, whatsoever things are honest, whatsoever things are just, whatsoever things are pure, whatsoever things are lovely, whatsoever things are of good report; if there be any virtue, and if there be any praise, think on these things"* (Philippians 4:8).

That is a guaranteed recipe for eliminating clutter from your mind. *"For God is not the author of confusion, but of peace"* (1 Corinthians 14:33).

Meditation places power in your hands. You can say, "Satan, I will no longer worry about what you have tried to deposit in my mind. I am going to focus on what God has already told me – that I am free!"

THREE OPINIONS

You are not what you think you are – you are what you think! The image is based on how you perceive yourself. That is why I say there are three opinions that matter:

One: Your opinion of God.

Two: God's opinion of you.

Three: Your opinion of yourself.

Satan desires to influence your thoughts because that is where your identity is located.

If the devil can make you think you are a failure, you will behave like one – even though you are not.

Remember, Satan does not need to control your action – he only needs to influence your thinking. He programs the computer of your mind so that the results will be the same even after he has left the scene.

Satan knows that if he enslaves one generation, he has won. Why? Because seed produces after its kind.

THE MAN WHO WINS

Several years ago someone gave me these thought-provoking words by an unknown author. They greatly inspired me at the time – and continue to give me guidance:

If you think you are beaten, you are,
If you think you dare not, you don't.
If you like to win, but you think you can't,
It is almost certain you won't.

If you think you'll lose, you're lost,
For out in the world we find,
Success begins with a fellow's will.
It's all in the state of mind.

If you think you are outclassed, you are,
You've got to think high to rise,
You've got to be sure of yourself before
You can ever win a prize.

Life's battles don't always go
To the stronger or faster man.
But soon or late the manwho wins,
Is the man who thinks he can.

Dr. Bronner's Checklist:

✓ When God permeates your life, you will react without a struggle.

✓ Beware of wrong mind-patterns. They can result in wrong action.

✓ Ask the Lord for help. You may be surprised at the results.

✓ Meditate on God's Word – day and night.

- ✓ If the devil can make you think you are a failure, you will behave like one.
- ✓ Start thinking like a champion.

Who is the man who wins? The man who thinks he can !

4

✓ CHECK YOUR WORDS

One of the great spiritual experiences of my life occurred in 1977. The Lord, along with two larger-than-life angels, appeared to me in my bedroom.

The angels stood at attention at the head of my bed on both sides.

My Bible was on the night stand and Jesus said, "Hold it up to your ear."

When I followed His command, He asked, "What do you hear?"

The Lord knew my response in advance and continued, "I know you don't hear anything."

I opened the Word and was directed to this verse: *"Bless the Lord, you His angels, Who excel in strength, who do His word, Heeding the voice of His word"* (Psalm 103:20 NKJV).

I looked again at the angels – at lease nine feet tall. "Who are they?" I wondered.

The Lord explained to me, "According to My word in Hebrews 1:14, these are ministering spirits sent to you because you are an heir of salvation. They hearken unto the voice of God's Word."

Then the Lord explained why I could hear nothing. He spoke, saying, "The Word will have no voice unless you place it into your heart and speak it."

From that moment forward I knew I was commanded by God to verbally share the message of Christ. I also realized that these angels were there to perform God's word which I voiced with my mouth! I understand that positive words in line with God's will would put these angels to work for me, but negative words would call them from duty.

CHOOSE CAREFULLY

Creation was the result of the spoken word. *"God said, Let there be light: and there was light"* (Genesis 1:3).

In fact, our entire universe was put into order by the voice of the Almighty: *"Through faith we understand that the worlds were framed by the word of God"* (Hebrews 11:3).

It is also true of you and me. Our world is fashioned by the words we utter. That is why we need to be extremely careful of what we say – and what we allow to come into our hearing.

Words are more than a medium of our expression; they are spiritual.

The same spirit God who used words to create everything that we see, is still at work. Even today, He gives us unique abilities and insights and allows us to write books, poems and songs.

However, just as the Holy Spirit speaks with words, so do demons. So people fail to recognize the voice of God, yet they are acutely attuned to everything Satan tells them. More than once, an accused murderer has declared to a jury, "A voice told me to kill those people."

Choose your words carefully! *"Death and life are in the power of the tongue"* (Proverbs 18:21). Satan does not respond to your thoughts, he responds to your words. That's why the only offensive weapon of the Christians armor is the *"sword of the Spirit, which is the word of God"* (Ephesians 6:17).

The sword is the "Word of God." That "word" is the Greek term "rhema" (spoken Word), not logos (the written Word). So the Word must be spoken for its power to be released.

SOWING AND REAPING

The Bible tells us, *"Let no corrupt communication proceed out of your mouth, but that which is good to the use of edifying, that it may minister grace unto the hearers"* (Ephesians 4:29).

Corrupt communication is truth spoken without grace. For example, I once heard someone called a "whore" and a "slut." Perhaps they were at one time. So the person was speaking truth – yet did not take into consideration the grace of God that had since come into their lives.

Don't let anybody bring you under condemnation based on your past. As a believer, you have been vindicated – washed by His Word and cleansed by His blood.

Some are quick to accuse and say, "Here is what he did. And this is where it happened!"

By placing their fingerprints where yours used to be, they now become guilty of the same thing from which God has set you free!

That is why Jesus said, *"Judge not, that ye be not judged"* (Matthew 7:1).

When you sow wickedness by attempting to impugn another's character, beware of the consequences. The Bible teaches, *"Be not deceived; God is not mocked: for whatsoever a man soweth, that shall he also reap"* (Galatians 6:7).

Carefully guard what you say because it is the source of both blessing and cursing. Jesus declared that it is *"Not what goes into the mouth [that] defiles a man; but what comes out of the mouth, this defiles a man"* (Matthew 15:11).

"STICKS AND STONES"

If you question whether words really have an effect on you, think again. We glibly recite, "Sticks and stones may break my bones, but words will never hurt me" – wrong!

Job cried, "How long will ye vex my soul, and break me in pieces with words?" (Job 19:2)

You may put on a brave face and remark, "I don't care what you say about me." Behind closed doors it's another story. You feel the pain and sob, "Lord, why?"

When a young man tells his girlfriend, "I think it is best that we begin to see other people. Let's just be friends," the words are often devastating. One woman recalled, "It was like I had been slapped. It really hurt me."

WORD CURSES

In the Sermon on the Mount, Jesus said, *"...whosoever shall say to his brother, Raca, shall be in danger of the council: but whosoever shall say, Thou fool, shall be in danger of hell fire"* (Matthew 5:22).

Raca is an Aramaic term of contempt. A fool, however is, a person who is good for nothing.

It is dangerous to call one of God's creations a fool. You are implying the Almighty has made a mistake – and you will be in danger of eternal punishment.

Word curses plague your mind and torment your soul. When a person offends or angers you by what they say, it is as though they pierced you. Later, when they apologize, the offense may be retracted but the wound remains.

Like the cut of a razor-sharp Knife, our words can be lethal.

The psalmist wrote, *"Hide me from the secret plots of the wicked, from the rebellion of the workers of iniquity, who sharpen their tongue like a sword, and bend their bows to shoot their arrows – bitter words"* (Psalm 64:2-3 NKJV).

Even the idle chatter we call gossip can deeply injure us. *"The words of a talebearer are like tasty trifles, and they go down into the inmost body"* (Proverbs 18:8 NKJV).

THE REAL YOU

When you deeply believe in – whether good or bad – will find a path to your lips. As Paul wrote, *"...we also believe, and therefore speak"* (2 Corinthians 4:13).

Our words are an outward expression of an inward condition.

- If we are filled with pessimism, we will have negative speech.
- If we are filled with gossip, we will share it.
- If we are filled with the Love of Jesus, we will tell the world about the Savior.

The Bible says, *"...for out of the abundance of the heart the mouth speaketh"* (Matthew 12:34).

LET YOUR MIND SPEAK

If you are in a situation where you cannot speak out loud, learn how to communicate with your mind. More than once, in my thoughts I have spoken, "The devil is a liar! I am blessed and highly favored of the Lord."

Learn how to tune your surroundings out.

I was praying in the sanctuary one afternoon and a musician who was rehearsing said, "Oh excuse me, Pastor. I didn't realize you were here. Is the music bothering you?"

"What music?" I honestly replied.

I was listening to the beat of a different drummer; His words had another cadence for me.

"THREE TIMES"

Here is a great principle we can learn from Jesus: Whatever you believe, speak it three times as much.

It is demonstrated in these words of the Master: *"For assuredly, I say to you, whoever says to this mountain, 'Be removed and be cast into the sea, ' and does not doubt in his heart, but believe that those things he says will be done, he will have whatever he says"* (Mark 11:12 NKJV).

Belief is mentioned only once, yet three times Jesus refers to speaking: "whosoever says," "those things he says," and "whatever he says."

If you plan to receive, start talking!

As the Old Testament records, when Joseph had a dream he had to tell it. Scripture states that *"he told it [to] his brethren* (Genesis 37:5).

SAY IT!

When the Lord gives you a promise, share the good news with someone you trust – your family, a friends, or a prayer partner. Why? Because that is how you release your faith. You are activating what is necessary to bring the promise into manifestation.

Even our praise is designed to be verbal. You don't extol the Lord merely by clapping your hands. Scripture says, *"...let us offer the sacrifice of praise to God continually, that is, the fruit of our lips giving thanks to his name"* (Hebrews 13:15).

The Bible also declares, *"Let every thing that hath breath praise the Lord"* (Psalm 150:6).

Power and glory are birthed when we open our mouths and bless the Lord.

We need to express it!

LISTEN!

Just as you monitor the words you speak, you must also guard your hearing. It is much like a football game – half of the time you are carrying the ball, and the rest of the time you are protecting it. Speaking is the offense, and listening is the defense.

Protect your hearing!

Jesus declared, *"If any man have ears to hear, let him hear. And he said unto them, Take heed what ye hear: with what measure ye mete, it shall be measured to you: and unto you that hear shall more be given"* (Mark 4:23-24).

Do you have an ear-filter? Some people are confused because they took the advice of others whose lives were out of step with the Lord. How can you expect to absorb the lyrics of ungodly music without those words making a permanent impression on your mind? Just because it is published doesn't mean that it is fit for human consumption! Take heed to what you hear.

I read the tragic story of a teen who was found dead in his pickup truck. The lyrics of the song in his cassette player were about a "suicide solution."

He listened, and took his own life.

What we hear has consequences. For example, if you grew up with people constantly berating you – telling you how unattractive you were, the probable result would be a poor self-image and low self esteem.

However, if every day you were encouraged and complimented, it would not take long for your inferiority complex to be reversed.

HEARING AND HEARING

In the bible we are asked, *"How then shall they call on him in whom they have not believed? And how shall they believe in him of whom they have not heard? And how shall they hear without a preacher?"* (Romans 10:14).

If you are not hearing the right message, start preaching to yourself!

When the Word comes out of your mouth you will both speak and hear it. That is a powerful combination.

Faith does not come by having heard. It is present tense. Scripture tells us, *"So then faith cometh by hearing, and hearing by the word of God"* (Romans 10:17).

It is the continual voice of the Lord that produces results. Read that verse again and you will understand that faith comes by "hearing and hearing" – having the Word impact your life again and again.

I have met people whose enthusiasm skyrockets when God gives them a plan for their future. However, when they return home, they are often surrounded by doubt, criticism and negativity.

Before long, like a new tire that is suddenly punctured by a nail, the air seeps out and they become deflated. Suddenly, they wonder, "What happened to my faith?"

DON'T STOP THE FLOW!

You are not transformed by having your mind renewed, but by *"the renewing of your mind"* (Romans 12:2). It must be a perpetual process.

If you sever the influence of the Word you eventually become like any other sinner:

- You will fall away from prayer.
- You will make unrighteous decisions.
- You will drift back to your old ways.

That is why Satan desperately wants to stop the flow of spiritual information and keep you in the dark. God says, *"My people are destroyed for lack of knowledge"* (Hosea 4:6).

I have seen God miraculously deliver people from drugs, only to watch them grow cold and regress to their former life.

Stay in the Word! Listen to the voice of God! Keep in constant communion with the Father.

Dr. Bronner's Checklist:

- ✓ Verbally proclaim the message of Christ.
- ✓ Avoid corrupt communication.
- ✓ Words are an outward expression of an inward condition.
- ✓ When God speaks to you, share the good news.
- ✓ Filter everything that enters your hearing.
- ✓ The continuous voice of the Lord produces faith and belief.

Ask yourself: "What am I saying? What am I hearing?"

Your future depends on it.

5

✓ CHECK YOUR WILL

In the pre-Civil War days, an Underground Railroad was created to help slaves escape to freedom. It was neither underground or an actual railroad. In most cases, the passengers were hidden in covered wagons or carts with false bottoms and transported from one secret station to another.

With the help of over 3,000 "conductors," 100,000 salves fled to freedom.

Harriet Tubman was a legend in those days. She was an escaped slaved who earned the name "Moses," for the courageous way she led people to the promise land – including her own aged parents.

When some travelers raised second thoughts, Harriet would take out her pistol and say, "You are not going back on me."

The strong-willed woman reinforced their decision!

Do you recall what happened to the children of Israel? On

their journey, they complained, *"Oh, that we had died by the hand of the Lord in the land of Egypt, when we sat by the pots of meat and when we ate bread to the full! For you have brought us out into this wilderness to kill this whole assembly with hunger"* (Exodus 16:3).

God had a divine will and purpose for their future and parted the waters so they could go forward. Then he closed the sea so they could not return!

"WHO TOUCHED ME?"

The strongest assertion that you can make in the English language is "I Will." When you make a final determination the results have no limits.

Once, when Jesus was on the way to the home of Jairus, to pray for his dying daughter, multitudes thronged around Him.

In the crowd was a woman who had been bleeding for twelve years. She had visited many physicians and had paid them well, yet instead of getting better her condition only deteriorated.

The woman had heard about Jesus, so she came up behind Him in the crowd and reached out to touch the hem of His garment. She said to herself, *"If I may touch but his clothes, I shall be whole"* (Mark 5:28).

She had already set her will to be healed before she ever touched Jesus. There was not an "if" or a "maybe." She was saying, "Let me just feel His garment and I will be healed."

The minute she did, God's supernatural power left Jesus and

flowed directly into the woman. Instantly, the bleeding stopped.

Scripture records that Jesus, *"...immediately knowing in himself that virtue had gone out of him, turned him about in the press, and said. Who touched my clothes?"*(Mark 5:30).

The disciples responded by asking, "With this large crowd around you, how can you ask, 'Who touched me?"

However, Jesus kept looking to see who had reached out to Him.

The woman, trembling at the realization that she had been healed, fell at the feet of Jesus and told him what she had done.

The Lord said to her, *"Daughter, thy faith hath made thee whole; go in peace, and be whole of they plague"* (Mark 5:34).

MORE THAN A "WANT"

If you desire to see a dramatic turn-around in your life, change your "want to" to a "will to."

Stop saying, "I *want* to have a greater relationship with the Lord" "I *want* to lose weight." Or, "I *want* to have more money."

Instead, confidently announce: "I *will* spend time in prayer and in the Word each morning." "I *will* lose 20 pounds." "I *will* invest five percent of my income every week."

Let me tell you about a teenager in our church who said, "I want to go on a mission trip this summer, but I don't have the money."

"Money?" That's the least of your worries," I told her. "You have got to make up your mind that you will be going!"

Once she made the decision, I knew she would find a way. I told her, "You may have to get an extra job, sell one of your possessions, or ask for a few sponsors, but you will go on that trip! And she did.

HE FOUND A WAY

I once interviewed a man for a job. "Do you have transportation?" I wanted to know.

"No, I don't own a car," was his answer.

That was not what I asked. "I don't care whether you have an automobile or not. Do you have a neighbor who will give you a ride, or can you get here on a city bus?"

It could have taken him a year to save for a car, but I needed his help immediately. The man understood and said, "I'll find a way. You can count on me. I will be here!"

UNDER CONTROL!

It is your resolve and determination that keeps you focused on course you have set. Here are five areas your will controls:

1. *Your will controls what you choose to believe.*
2. *Your will controls your level of commitment to any person or any project.*
3. *Your will controls the course on which your life is set.*

4. *Your will controls the degree of your obedience.*
5. *Your will controls the consistency of your character and your behavior.*

We were created as free moral agents. That means God will never override our natural human will. Not even Satan can supersede it.

The devil appeals to your wants. Then he tricks you into setting your determination based on those same desires. "Oh, look how handsome he is," tempts Satan. "Don't you want him?" he suggests.

You reply, "Yes – and I will do anything to get him."

That's how our wants steer us toward trouble.

ANGELS WILL ARRIVE

Here is an important principle: *Change is the product of human effort sustained by divine help.*

The moment you set your will, God will arrive on the scene and assist you.

We all know the story of Jesus and His death on the Cross, yet it was not His desire to endure such pain and agony. The flesh recoils from death.

In the Garden of Gethsemane, just before the crucifixion, Jesus *"...was withdrawn from them about a stone's throw, and He knelt down and prayed, saying, 'Father, if it is Your will, take this cup away from Me; nevertheless not My will, but Yours, be done'"*

(Luke 22:41-42 NKJV).

When Jesus spoke those words, He exchanged His desire for God's ultimate purpose.

What was the result? The Father sent help from above. *"Then an angel appeared to Him from heaven, strengthening Him"* (v.43).

What a marvelous God! The instant you submit to His will, He will dispatch angelic help on your behalf.

When you admit, "Lord, I am going through a difficult time, but I am aligning my will with Yours," supernatural aid is on the way.

To say, "Not my will, but Yours" represents a personal decision. Then God takes over.

MARY'S DECISION

In the city of Nazareth, a virgin named Mary was engaged to Joseph. An angel appeared with the news that she would conceive of the Holy Ghost, and the child that *"...shall be born of thee shall be called the Son of God"* (Luke 1:35).

Mary was shocked at the news, yet she responded with these life-changing words. She looked up to heaven and declared, *"Behold the handmaid of the Lord; be it unto me according to thy word"* (v.38).

When she relinquished her will to the Father, a miraculous series of events unfolded that led to the birth of the Savior. Mary was undergirded with divine help.

SELF-CONTROL?

You may ask, "How can I know the perfect will of God?"

I am constantly amazed at how the Bible is still relevant today.

For example, an alcoholic or drug addict can read the Word and become convicted of their actions. You see, they are driven by their own will – because they want a temporary escape or desire to "get high."

The will of the Lord, however, is that we be "sober" and "vigilant" (1 Peter 5:8). Christ has *"granted unto us his precious and exceeding great promises; that through these ye may become partakers of the divine nature, having escaped from the corruption that is in the world* (2 Peter 1:4 NKJV). For this reason we are to exercise our faith by adding virtues including *"self-control"* (v.6).

Following the will of God isn't easy. You will say, "Lord, I don't know how I am going to do this. It is so difficult!"

When you make a spiritual decision to change, God will send the support you need.

CLAIM THE PROMISE

I spoke with a woman who received a disturbing medical report. What was her response? "The doctor said this runs in our family." Then she added, "I even had an aunt who died from the same condition."

Where was her faith? Where was the confidence that she would regain her health? The woman needed to be claiming God's promise: *"I will not die, but I will live and declare the works of the*

Lord" (Psalm 118:17).

As you speak those words faith begins to rise from within and God will intervene.

"WE WILL"

When you sincerely pray, "Lord, use me in Your service," He will send people your direction and present you with marvelous opportunities for ministry. You will become the answer to their needs.

Say, *"...as for me and my house, we will serve the Lord"* (Joshua 24:15).

Your commitment is not based on feelings or emotion. It's easy to proclaim. "I will bless the Lord," yet there are times when you are consumed with life's circumstances and just don't feel like praising Him. However, when your will is indelibly set, you will worship the Lord regardless of your situation. He is worthy of your praise!

With the psalmist you can declare, *"I will bless the Lord at all times: his praise shall continually be in my mouth"* (Psalms 34:1).

WHAT ABOUT ME?

The Lord has provided everything you need for spiritual success. The Bible declares that *"...his divine power hath given unto us all things that pertain unto life and godliness, through the knowledge of him that hath called us to glory and virtue"* (2 Peter 1:3).

You alone are in control of your will – the steering wheel of your life.

Then King Uzziah died, the people were not sure who would be their next leader. At the same time, Isaiah saw a vision of the Lord – *"...sitting on a throne, high and lifted up, and the train of His robe filled the temple"* (Isaiah 6:1 NKJV).

Isaiah, recognizing how unworthy he was in the presence of God, cried, *"Woe is me, for I am undone! Because I am a man of unclean lips"* (v.5).

Immediately, *"...one of the seraphim flew to me, having in his hand a live coal which he had taken with the tongs from the altar. And he touched my mouth with it, and said: 'Behold, this has touched your lips; Your iniquity is taken away, And your sin purged'"* (vv.6-7).

Then the Lord asked this important question: *"Whom shall I send, and who will go for Us?"* (v.8).

Isaiah didn't hesitate. He cried, *"Here am I! Send me"* (v.8).

The prophet was in control of his own will. The enemy could not prevent him from raising his hand in the Spirit, saying. "I will go! Send me!"

SUSTAINING POWER

Satan tries to stop us from accomplishing the Lord's purpose. He connives to discourage and derail us – to get us off track from the glorious things of God.

It's time to declare, "I will not be denied!"

Have the stamina and determination to say, "I don't care how long it takes, or what I must endure, I am going to stand firm and see God do great exploits in my life!"

You can make up your mind, yet if you don't have the sustaining power of the Lord your best intentions won't last.

It must be *His* will for us. God declares, *"For my thoughts are not your thoughts, neither are your ways my ways, saith the Lord. For as the heavens are higher than the earth, so are my ways higher than your ways, and my thoughts than your thoughts"* (Isaiah 55:8-9).

The key to victory is to parallel our thoughts with God's. That is how you will know His purpose.

Dr. Bronner's Checklist:

- ✓ Make certain your will lines up with God's will.
- ✓ Change your "want to" to a "will to."
- ✓ Your will determines what you choose to believe.
- ✓ Change is the product of human effort sustained by divine help.
- ✓ You alone are in control of your will.
- ✓ Make God's thoughts your thoughts.

Your will represents the most powerful, formidable natural human force on the earth. When it is in harmony with the will of God, nothing is impossible.

6

✓ CHECK YOUR DECISION MAKING

Every choice we make in life is accompanied by this question: *How much pain or pleasure is this going to cost me?*

If there is not significant effort or discomfort associated with the process, we will not appreciate the delight.

At our church, I insist that every service begins on time because I associate being late with pain. Why? A late start punishes people for being punctual and rewards those who are tardy. I refuse to do it!

It is a lesson we all need to learn. Let me tell you a secret about people who are habitually late for work, for church or for appointments. They usually have less than perfect credit because they don't pay their bills on time! Ouch!

OUR CHOICES

The pleasure/pain principle is found in Scripture. Read Deuteronomy 28 and you will find a complete chapter on the blessing and cursing of the Lord. Notice how it is divided: the first 14 verses deal exclusively with blessing, while the reaming 54 verses concern curses.

At one point God said the result of disobedience would be that He shall *"...smite thee in the knees, and in the legs, with a sore botch that cannot be healed, from the sole of thy foot unto the top of thy head"* (Deuteronomy 28:35).

I believe the Lord wanted to paint a picture so graphic that it would drive us away from what is forbidden.

The Creator designed us so that we will gravitate toward what brings us pleasure, and move away from that which would bring pain.

JOY IS WAITING!

Many of the good things God has ordained for us require suffering for their achievement. For example, there is tremendous pain during childbirth, but the mother says, "I am willing to endure the agony because I know there will be such happiness ahead."

Christ saw the glory that was waiting *beyond* Calvary. That is how He was able to accept the nails in His hands and thorns on his brow. As the writer of Hebrews tells us, we are to look unto Jesus, *"...who for the joy that was set before him endured the cross, despising the shame, and is set down at the right hand of the throne of God"* (Hebrews 12:2).

We need to use His experiences to give ourselves a mental checkup. *"For consider him that endured such contradiction of sinners against himself, lest ye be wearied and faint in your minds"* (Hebrews 12:3).

AVOIDING PAIN

To move away from something harmful we must associate discomfort with it. Here are three ways we learn to avoid pain:

FIRST: WE LEARN FROM EXPERIENCE.

A child who sticks his hand on a hot stove instantly learns a life-changing lesson. He is unlikely to touch it again!

Perhaps you will have a confrontation with someone who causes you great heartache. The pain of that ordeal will hopefully prompt you to say, "I don't want any more of that!"

The psalmist explained the results of experience when he wrote, *"Create in me a clean heart, O God; and renew a right spirit within me. Cast me not away from thy presence; and take not thy holy spirit from me. Restore unto me the joy of thy salvation; and uphold me with thy free spirit. Then will I teach transgressors thy ways; and sinners shall be converted unto thee"* (Psalm 51:10-13).

SECOND: WE LEARN FROM REPULSIVE IMAGES.

When one of the choices you are about to make is associated with a mental picture of something deplorable, even disgusting, you will likely make the right decision.

When we see something frightful we want to steer clear and

back away from it.

I believe every teen who contemplates using hard drugs needs to have a face to face meeting with an addict whose pallor is pasty, whose eyes are glazed over and whose mind is fried. Perhaps then they will say, "If this is my future, I'm stopping now!"

THIRD: WE LEARN FROM IMPACT TESTIMONIES.

I talked to a young man who, after getting in trouble with the law, was taken to a state prison "just for a tour." Some of the inmates were asked to tell him what it was really like behind bars. "Man, you don't want to come here," they told him. "You'll be fresh meat – and I guarantee you'll be knifed and raped!"

It made an incredible lasting impact on the teen.

Similarly, you don't have to become a smoker to understand the hazards of cigarettes. Thousands who are dying of lung cancer can warn you, "Don't ever put nicotine in your mouth. Look what happened to me!"

Hopefully you'll be scared straight and say, "I'm never touching the stuff!"

A personal declaration can make a difference!

THE PROCESS

When you are about to make a decision, take a piece of paper and divide it in two columns: Advantages/ Disadvantages. Then write your lists.

Before a person decides to quit smoking, they need to

conclude cigarettes cause more harm than good. What would they list as pleasures? The person may decide, "It relaxes my nerves, curbs my appetite, and I think it makes me look cool!"

What are the liabilities? Cancer, respiratory problems, dark lips, yellow teeth, bad breath, foul smelling clothes and hair, high blood pressure, and the destruction of your B vitamins that help you cope with stress. Plus, cigarettes are terribly expensive. Only by comparing both sides can you make a rational decision.

It's also true of our diet.

You walk through the cafeteria line and drool, "Look at that fried pork – and apple pie. I've got to have some of that!"

There is great satisfaction in food, yet we need to face the dangers of overeating and the risk of harmful ingredients. Heart disease, high blood pressure, back problems and strokes – not to mention indigestion, guilt and outgrowing your wardrobe – are a few of the drawbacks.

When you think about a diabetic who must shoot insulin into their veins every day, you might want to say, "That cake and ice cream baptized in fudge sure is tasty, but is it good enough for me to wind up sticking needles in my body?"

You need to reach the point where you decide, "I am not going to allow anything to short-circuit my life and rob me of my destiny."

Declare, "I will not let my cravings cripple my body and place me in the hospital where I pay exorbitant medical bills trying to stay healthy."

It is your choice!

THE POWER OF LOVE

What draws us close to the Lord and compels us to do the right thing? It is the love of God. As Paul wrote, *"Though I speak with the tongues of men and of angels, but have not love, I have become sounding brass or clanging cymbal"* (1 Corinthians 13:1 NKJV).

God has placed both love and fear inside us for a reason. The first is to draw us to Himself; the second is to keep us away from everything that is unlike Him.

"IS IT WORTH IT?"

When Satan lures us, he never shows us the pain. In the Garden of Eden, the serpent didn't tell Eve what would happen if she took a bite of the forbidden fruit. He promoted the benefits, then lied, saying, *"Ye shall not surely die"* (Genesis 3:4). But what about the consequences?

The devil is using the same old tricks today. He says "Look at that man's car! Look at his house!" –not telling you about the debt trap that is about to ensnare you.

What good is fleeting pleasure when the pain and guilt will rob you of your relationship with God? Is it worth is?

You need to decide, "Lord, I will follow You regardless of the suffering and persecution I may encounter." Jesus said, "And ye shall be hated of all men for my name's sake: but he that shall endure unto the end, the same shall be saved" (Mark 13:13).

FIVE VITAL FACTORS

Your choices determine everything – your conduct, your character and your future. Let's look at five important factors that govern your decision making:

1. YOUR EMOTIONAL STATE.

The sales person at the dress shop comments, "Oh that looks so good on you." Flattered, you purchase it, whether you have the money or not.

Any woman who suffers with PMS will understand that we can sometimes operate from an emotional state. Well, men also go through PMS – *Power, Money and Sex*. Those things can contribute to rash decisions.

Jesus taught us: *"Let not your heart be troubled"* (John 14:1).

He was saying, "You are in charge of your emotions – do not allow your feelings to control you."

The next time you feel dejected and "bent out of shape," snap out of it!

The Bible says, *"Set your affection on things above"* (Colossians 3:2). Firmly set them! – don't be indecisive, vacillating back and forth.

2. THE QUESTION YOU ASK.

If you are going to make a rational, intelligent decision, you had better examine the options. Ask:

- How much will this cost me?
- What is the downside?
- Is this in line with my destiny?

Taking a second job may be the right thing for you, yet before taking that option you need to ask, "Is the time I will be away from my family worth the trade-off? Is money the real issue? Why is this important to me? Will it enhance my career plan?"

To find the best answers, ask the right questions!

3. YOUR MENTOR REFERENCES.

To build accountability into your life, have individuals who are your role models and set the standards for your behavior.

They are your mentor references.

Just before making a decision ask yourself, "What would my spouse say about this? What would be my employer's opinion? What would my teacher think?"

You may even wonder. "If my mother were still alive, how would she handle this situation?" Better yet, WWJD? – What Would Jesus Do?

If you are submitted to leadership, ask, "How would he or she respond?" – and the wisdom of the anointing in that person's life will flow into yours."

It is important to have a specific "life coach" so you will be in a mentor-prote'ge' relationship. Your decisions will change for the better because of the sense of responsibility you feel. Plus, you will want to make you advisor proud you. It is a win-win situation.

4. YOUR DATA BANK.

Remember, knowledge is power – and you make the best decisions when you have a continuous flow of the right information.

The person who spends just thirty minutes a day studying the same topic will become among the world's leading authorities on that subject in their lifetime!

Some of the best Bible teachers I have ever listened to have never spent a day in college or attended seminary. They learned everything by a personal, daily study of the Word. Then they applied it to their lives.

Don't laugh at people who place verses of Scripture and nuggets of wisdom on their mirror or refrigerator door. What goes in comes out! And if you are filled with the right information, you will make much wiser choices.

5. YOUR VALUE SYSTEM.

Earlier in this book we discussed your core beliefs – and they are essential in making life choices.

Every decision is linked to your spiritual values, and you must constantly ask, "What do I feel in my heart about this matter? It is contrary to my commitment to the Lord?"

As a believer you are a representative of the King of Kings and Lord of Lords. Are your actions the reflection of a child of God?

Be like David, who told the Lord, *"Thy word have I hid in mine heart, that I might not sin against thee"* (Psalm 119:1).

"SHOULD I?"

The longer you stay on God's prescribed course, the easier it is to make the right decisions. When temptation looms you won't have to wonder, "Should I, or shouldn't I?" You will instantly know the answer. The Lord says, *"Behold, I set before you the way of life, and the way of death"* (Jeremiah 21:8).

Once you have made what you believe is a God-inspired, wise choice, stick with it! What is the benefit of enrolling in a Bible Study, a diet program or setting a family budget if you fail to follow through?

Make your choices with prayer, and make them permanent!

Dr Bronner's Checklist:

- ✓ Ask, "How much pain or pleasure will this cost me?"
- ✓ We learn to avoid suffering by experience, from repulsive images and impact testimonies.
- ✓ Don't allow the pleasure of the moment to rob you of your relationship with the Lord.

- ✓ Do not let emotion be the reason for your decision.
- ✓ Make choices based on you mentor references.
- ✓ Every option must be linked to your spiritual values.

Making decisions is much like finding honey – you may have to fight the bees! But think of the pleasure you will eventually receive!

7

✓ CHECK YOUR VISION

Like a digital camera, our mind remembers things in picture form. That is why, when someone hasn't seen you in a long time, they often say, "Oh, I remember your face, but I can't place your name."

The person may even recall when and where they last saw you, reciting all the details. Yet because they didn't see your name it escapes their memory.

I was speaking with a man who had been reading the same copy of his old Bible and was trying to locate a particular verse. He said, "I don't know exactly where that verse is, but it's on the right side of the page, about two-thirds down."

In his mind's eye he could see it, but couldn't quote it!

THE SOURCE OF WORDS

Listen closely to a conversation and you might hear someone ask, "Do you see what I am saying?"

Think about that phrase for a moment and here is what you will realize: *you can never say it unless you envision it.* It is our mental image that produces words. We say exactly what we see!

When God births something in my spirit, I don't have to read it – only describe it.

There is a certain level of faith that will never be stimulated until you visualize what God is saying to you.

Meditate on the Word until it becomes alive – until it creates pictures in your mind, soul and heart. When that day arrives Scripture will truly begin to speak to you, and you will never forget it!

"WITH MY OWN EYES!"

In most cases, we don't actually believe something until we have seen it personally.

The queen of Sheba heard the incredible stories of the temple Solomon had built. She decided to make an official visit and, after a lavish banquet, told the king, *"It was a true report which I heard in my own land about your words and your wisdom. However I did not believe the words until I came and saw with my own eyes; and indeed the half was not told me. Your wisdom and prosperity exceed the face of which I heard.* (I Kings 10:6-7) NKJV).

Seeing is believing!

"LOOK UP!"

God used visualization to instill faith in Abraham. He revealed something that inspired the man who would become the father of the nations.

The Lord had given him a verbal promise and declared, "I am going to bless you," but for Abraham that was abstract.

Here was a man who was childless, yet God promised that he was going to have so many children he wouldn't know how to count them!

Abraham did not truly comprehend what the Lord was saying until one clear night when God asked him to, "Look up!" Then He asked, "Do you see those stars?"

"Yes," said Abraham, "but there are so many!"

The Lord replied, "That is how large your family will be!"

Here is how Scripture describes the scene. "He brought him outside and said, 'Look now toward heaven, and count the stars if you are able to number them.' And He said to him, 'So shall your descendants be'" (Genesis 15:5 NKJV).

STARS AND SAND

I believe, as Abraham stared into those stars, he saw the faces of his children, his grandchildren and great grandchildren – even before he ever had a child of his own.

Next, God said, "Now look down at the sand on the shore." On every grain I believe he saw his children – and those of generations yet to come. The Lord announced, *"That in blessing I will bless thee, and in multiplying I will multiply thy seed as the stars of the heaven, and as the sand which is upon the sea shore;*

and thy seed shall possess the gate of his enemies" (Genesis 22:17).

I can imagine Abraham shouting, "Lord, I can see it! I believe it!"

When he envisioned what the Lord proclaimed, faith stirred in his heart.

Remember this: what God shoes you in heaven, He will confirm on earth.

VISUALIZE IT!

You will never rise above the pictures that are engraved on your mind. How can a person expect to lose weight if all they see are rolls and wrinkles?

Instead, find a photo of yourself before you gained those extra pounds – and post it somewhere visible.

You may say, I've never been slim, there's no picture available.

Well, find a model in a magazine and paste your face over theirs! You must be able to *see it in order to be it.*

If you are a blue collar worker and you want to be "white collar," buy yourself a new shirt!

Take a photo of yourself in your finest suit and say, "There I am, on the cover of Success Magazine!"

If you want to see yourself dancing, put your picture on the face of a famous ballerina.

Do you have a dream of opening your own restaurant? Buy

a chef's hat and an apron, and take a snapshot. Every day, take a look at the person you are going to become.

Before he got his first break as an actor, Jim Carey wrote a check to himself for $10 million, signed it and said, "One day I am going to be able to cash you!"

Don't just verbalize it, visualize it.

WHAT WILL IT BE?

Do you have an image of what the Lord desires for you?

- If your body is sick, you must see yourself well!
- If your wallet is empty, you must see it full!
- If your children have strayed from God, you must see them saved!

Stop dwelling on what *is*. Today, you may be dealing with a child who doesn't seem to have any ambition and fails to obey.

Get a new picture. Blank out that negative view and see him at a graduation ceremony – proudly walking down the aisle, dressed in a flowing robe with a tassel on his cap.

If you only dwell on what already exists, you will miss what God wants to bring into reality.

A WRITTEN STRATEGY

Regardless of what you are struggling with, here are two vital steps you must take:

1. *Decide how you will overcome the problem.*

2. *Write a goal plan to achieve it.*

Design a strategy, create a paradigm, build a model, fashion to prototype, draw a sketch or make a list. Do whatever it takes to bring your dream to life. If it is a stronghold of debt, create a plan to become financially free.

Read your written objectives daily.

Don't just scribble a note, then hide it in a drawer. *Write the vision, read the vision, and run with it.* That is God's command to you (Habakkuk 2:3).

It has been said that a short pencil is worth more than a long memory!

YOUR SOURCE OF HOPE

You don't have the chance to exercise personal discipline unless your future is more important than your present circumstances.

The goal in front of you must take precedence over the temptation that is after you.

Do you know why people backslide? It is because they don't think their spiritual future is more attractive than their sinful past. So they switch their gears to "reverse!"

It is foresight that gives you the power to walk away from what is behind you. And what is the source of that inspiration? The psalmist said it best when he wrote, *"My soul, wait thou only upon God; for my expectation is from him"* (Psalms 62:5).

Only the Lord can give you a hope-filled future.

DO IT!

Speaking is vital, and so is listening. However, there is something about seeing an object that inscribes it indelibly on your mind. Job said to the Lord, *"I have heard of You by the hearing of the ear, but now my eye sees You"* (Job 42:5).

The reason Scripture tells us to meditate night and day is so that we may "observe to do all that is written therein" (Joshua 1:8).

The Lord wants us to see what is in the Word.

One thing more. We are to add legs to our sight – we are to do it.

Paul gave us a wonderful list (including truth, love, and things that are of good report), then said, "think on these things" (Philippians 4:8). The next verse, however, is equally significant. We are told, *"Those things, which ye have both learned, and received, and heard, and seen in me, do: and the God of peace shall be with you"* (Philippians 4:9).

In those two verses you have a six path to success:

1. Think it!
2. Learn it!
3. Receive it!
4. Hear it!
5. See it!
6. Do it!

The purpose of the first five steps is to propel your life into action. That is what puts the "Go" in Gospel.

Dr. Bronner's Checklist:

- ✓ You will never rise above the pictures engraved on your mind.
- ✓ What God shows you in heaven He will confirm on earth.
- ✓ Stop dwelling on what is and see what will be.
- ✓ Write your vision!
- ✓ The goal in front of you must take precedence over the temptation that is behind you.
- ✓ Add legs to your sight!

God desires that we enlarge our vision, however, nothing can prepare us for what lies ahead. *"Eye hath not seen, nor ear heard, neither have entered into the heart of man, the things which God hath prepared for them that love him"* (1 Corinthians 2:9).

What a day that will be!

8

✓ CHECK YOUR WEAPONS

It is foolish to go into battle without being properly equipped. Scripture tells us that *"...the weapons of our warfare are not carnal, but mighty through God"* (2 Corinthians 10:4).

As we will see, the equipment the Lord provides for the conflict may seem strange to the unbeliever, yet it is mighty in His sight.

God will give you a divine strategy that will astound the enemy. He can take what is little and magnify it!

LITTLE IS MUCH

One of my favorite accounts in the Old Testament concerns four lepers who were outside the city gates. They said to one another, *"Why are we sitting here until we die? If we say, 'We will enter the city,' the famine is in the city, and we shall die there. And if we sit here, we die also. Now therefore, come, let shall live; and if they kill us, we shall only die"* (2 Kings 7:3-4 NKJV).

When they reached the Syrian camp the lepers were surprised to find no one there. Why? The Lord had *"caused the army of the Syrians to hear the noise of chariots and the noise of horses – the noise of a great army"* (v.6).

I believe God amplified the sounds of the lepers as they walked. It must have sounded like 300,000 men. The enemy ran for their lives, and the lepers feasted on the spoils.

Don't belittle the weapons God places in your hands. He will increase them if you lift Him up.

In the words of the psalmist, *"O magnify the Lord with me, and let us exalt his name together"* (Psalm 34:3).

The battle is not ours. It is the Lord's – and He will fight for us.

CARNAL WEAPONS

In the natural we want to attack with the equipment of the world – carnal weapons.

One man told me, "Sometimes I feel like laying my religion down and giving them a piece of my mind!" He wanted to wage war using his *old* nature.

Vindictiveness and retaliation are not the ways God intends for His children to wage this warfare.

Before we discuss the spiritual ammunition the Lord desires that we use, let's discuss eight carnal weapons:

CARNAL WEAPON NUMBER ONE: REASON

Scientific inquiry may use inductive or deductive reasoning, yet it is not a spiritual weapon.

Attempting to rationalize or analyze issues can destroy your spiritual foundation. Human logic will try to convince you, "This does not make sense. Why do you spend so much time praying for a miracle when it isn't going to happen?" However, the person who has been healed doesn't worry about analysis; they have the evidence!

If you become convinced you can reason your way through problems, you will eventually place your trust and confidence in self, not in God. Your salvation is based on faith – *"the substance of things hoped for, the evidence of things not seen"* (Hebrews 11:1).

CARNAL WEAPON NUMBER TWO: ARGUMENT

I have seen long-standing friendship dissolve because of a disagreement over some minor issue. "I can't even remember what we were squabbling about," one man told me, "but he hasn't spoken to me since!"

Paul addressed the topic when he wrote, *"If anyone...does not consent to wholesome words, even the words of our Lord Jesus Christ, and to the doctrine which accords with godliness, he is proud, knowing nothing, but is obsessed with disputes and arguments over words, from which com envy, strife, reviling, evil suspicions, useless wranglings"* (1 Timothy 6:3-5 NKJV).

Don't allow discord and controversy to rob you of God's blessing.

CARNAL WEAPON NUMBER THREE: BRIBES

When I was a guest chaplain at the Georgia State Senate, one person introduced himself and said, "I am a lobbyist" – and named the large company he represented."

Later I thought about his work and concluded that in many cases lobbying is a sophisticated, legalized, acceptable form of bribery. "What can I give you to secure your vote?"

Some people even try bribing God. "Lord, they say, "If you will heal my daughter, I will start paying tithes." Or, "Lord, I am not going to eat until You send me a husband!" How foolish! God knows *"your mighty sins; they afflict the just, they take a bribe"* (Amos 5:12).

CARNAL WEAPON NUMBER FOUR: INTIMIDATION

We become concerned when a child is "bullied" in school, yet the same tactics are practiced by adults every day. Some people get their kicks out of intimidating everyone in sight and displaying their aggressive personality.

You can recognize carnal people because they use these fleshly weapons-including threats and harassment.

"You don't want to mess with me!" they say. "You do that and I'll be talking with you in court."

Being a Christian means to be "Christ-like," and Jesus said, *"Do not intimidate anyone or accuse falsely"* (Luke 3:14 NKJV).

Don't mistake meekness for weakness! It is a sign of spiritual strength.

CARNAL WEAPON NUMBER SIX: WORRY OR DOUBT

How does a mind filled with anxiety and apprehension have room to receive God's blessing? It can't! We must empty ourselves of fear and doubt before the Lord can re-fill us.

Worry expects the worst to happen – while faith expects the best. The two concepts are in conflict with each other. Jesus warned that *"the cares of this world"* can *"choke the word"* and it becomes unfruitful (Mark 4:19).

The key to faith is total belief. The Lord tells us that the person who *"says to this mountain, 'Be removed and cast in to the sea, 'and does not doubt in his heart...he will have whatever he says"* (Mark 11:23 NKJV).

CARNAL WEAPON NUMBER SEVEN: GUILT

Have you ever been put on a guilt trip?

A husband will complain, "Why didn't you buy the kind of steaks I like?" A child will pout, "Why did you throw away my favorite toy? Even worse, a person will say, "I have to forgive you for what you did to me!"

What is the objective? They want to make you feel guilty – to cause you to believe you owe them something!

The greatest cause of shame and remorse, however, is sin. Guilt is only the symptom.

Christ came to forgive us of our trespasses. To the woman

accused of adultery, Jesus said, *"Neither do I condemn thee: go, and sin no more"* (John 8:11). He removed the shame from her life.

CARNAL WEAPONS NUMBER EIGHT: UNFORGIVENESS

Harboring grudges and resentment is like holding a hand grenade with the pin pulled. You know it will explode! That's why the topic of forgiveness is a recurring theme of Scripture.

Failure to pardon the transgressions of others can result in unwanted consequences. Like a boomerang, the offense might become yours. Jesus taught, *"If you forgive the sins of any, they are forgiven them; if you retain the sins of any, they are retained"* (John 20:23 NKJV). By embracing someone's iniquities, you actually possess them in you – and become a partaker in the sin.

How can the problem be resolved? *"Forgive, and ye shall be forgiven"* (Luke 6:37).

SPIRITUAL WEAPONS

What a contrast there is between the weapons of the flesh and those of the Spirit!

David fought Goliath with more than a slingshot and five stones. He had the power of the Almighty on His side.

Gideon went to battle with a small band of men armed only with pitchers, lamps and trumpets. Yet, when they shouted, *"The sword of the Lord, and of Gideon* (Judges 7:20), a vast army was defeated.

Today, *"we wrestle not against flesh and blood, but against principalities, against powers, against the rulers of the darkness of this world, against spiritual wickedness in high places"* (Ephesians 6:12)

To become victorious, use these eight mighty weapons:

SPIRITUAL WEAPON NUMBER ONE: THE NAME OF JESUS

As a believer, the most commanding, authoritative words you will ever utter are these: " In the name of Jesus!"

You have been given power of attorney to cast out devils and declare healing. What an awesome weapon!

The name of Jesus is the highest designation in heaven or on earth. *"Wherefore God also heath highly exalted him, and given him a name which is above every name"* (Philippians 2:9).

It is saving name! *"Neither is there salvation in any other: for there is none other name under heaven given among men, whereby we must be saved"* (Acts 4:12).

Whatever we do – in word or in deed – *"do all in the name of the Lord Jesus"* (Colossians 3:17).

SPIRITUAL WEAPON NUMBER TWO: THE BLOOD OF JESUS

A woman told me her unforgettable encounter with a man who raped her. "What did you do?" I asked.

She said, ""My grand mother told me that if I was ever in a dangerous situation I should plead the blood of Jesus. And that is exactly what I did. I cried out 'The blood of Jesus! The blood of

Jesus!'"

I was startled at what happened next. "The man died on top of me!" she testified. The Lord came to her rescue! When the blood that Christ shed on the Cross is applied to your life there is both protection and salvation. The writer of Hebrews declared, *"...without shedding of blood is no remission"* (Hebrews 9:22).

It is God's *"everlasting covenant"* (Hebrews 13:20).

SPIRITUAL WEAPON NUMBER THREE: GOD'S WORD

When God wants something supernatural to occur in your life He will speak through His Word to your spirit. Scripture will begin to say:

- "Fear not my child! Be not afraid for I am with thee."
- "No weapon formed against you shall prosper."
- "This sickness is not unto death!"

The Lord will give you exactly what you need at that moment. At the time of temptation in the wilderness, Jesus said to the devil, *"It is written, Man shall not live by bread alone, but by every word that proceedeth out of the mouth of God"* (Matthew 4:4).

It was the Word that caused Satan to flee!

SPIRITUAL WEAPON NUMBER FOUR: PRAYER

A father, telling me about his wayward son, lamented, "Pastor, I have tried everything. He just won't straighten up!"

"I believe I know something that will work," I told him. "Why don't you try prayer?"

When you call on the Lord, He will make a way where there seems no way.

God not only hears your prayer, He answers! The Lord *"will be very gracious unto thee at the voice of thy cry; when he shall hear it, he will answer thee"* (Isaiah 30:19).

Don't be impatient. The psalmist said, *"I waited patiently for the Lord; and he inclined unto me, and heard my cry"* (Psalm 40:1-2).

Nothing can be a substitute for persistent prayer.

SPIRITUAL WEAPON NUMBER FIVE: FAITH

"If I just had more faith, I could defeat the enemy!" I've heard people say. According to the Word, even a smidgen of faith is powerful in the sight of God. When the apostles asked the Lord to increase their belief, He declared, *"If you have faith as a mustard seed, you can say to this mulberry tree, 'Be pulled up by the roots and be planted in the sea.' And it would obey you"* (Luke 17:6 NKJV).

Jesus was saying, "You do not need more faith. Just use what you already have."

The next time you are confronted with an obstacle that seems insurmountable, start reading Hebrews, chapter 11. You'll learn that it was *by faith* great men and women of God were able to overcome.

SPIRITUAL WEAPON NUMBER SIX: LOVE

If you don't believe love is a weapon, think about the phrase, "Kill them with kindness!"

The greatest enemies of your live have the potential to become your friends when you shower them with the Father's love. There is no room for hatred in God's Kingdom. The Bible tells us *"If someone says, 'I love God,' and hates his brother, he is a liar; for he who does not love his brother whom he has seen, how can he love God whom he has not seen? And this commandment we have from Him: that he who loves God must love his brother also"* (1 John 4:20,21).

Let love with your battles!

SPIRITUAL WEAPONS NUMBER SEVEN: THE FEAR OF THE LORD

Many today don't fully understand the term, "The fear of the Lord." They think it means we should be frightened and cower in the presence of a God who rules with wrath and judgment.

Far from it! These words are used in Scripture to remind us the Lord deserves our respect, reverence, worship and fellowship. It is a fear that is joined with love and hope. The Bible tells us that the fear of the Lord:

- "is the beginning of wisdom" (Psalms 111:10).
- "is the beginning of knowledge" (Proverbs 1:7).
- "prolongs our days" (Proverbs 10:27).
- "is a fountain of life" (Proverbs 14:27).

I pray that we would be empowered by the same gifts found in the churches in Judea, Galilee and Samaria. Scripture records they *"were edified; and walking in the fear of the Lord, and in the comfort of the Holy Ghost"* (Acts 9:31).

SPIRITUAL WEAPON NUMBER EIGHT: DIVINE COVENANT

You can build a fortress of protection for your life when you come into a covenant relationship with the Lord.

God told Abraham, *"I establish my covenant with you, and with your seed after you"* (Genesis 9:9). The vow continued through his lineage of David and led to the birth of Christ.

As believers we inherit *"the blessing of Abraham...through Jesus Christ [and] receive the promise of the Spirit through faith"* (Galatians 3:14).

We remain in covenant with God by obeying His Word, supporting His work, and through communion with the Father.

It is also how we triumph in the conflict.

Dr. Bronner's Checklist:

✓ Allow the Lord to magnify your weapons.
✓ Don't let discord and controversy rob you of God's blessing.
✓ Do not mistake meekness for weakness.
✓ The name of Jesus gives you power of attorney.
✓ The Word will cause Satan to flee.
✓ Establish a covenant relationship with the Almighty.

With God pulling for us, and Satan pulling against us, we find ourselves in the center of an eternal skirmish. If you plan to triumph, sharpen your spiritual weapons.

✓ A POST-CHECKUP VISIT

The Lord doesn't give you a one-time examination and say "That's it! I don't ever need to see you again."

No. Our walk with God must be daily. As Paul wrote to young Timothy, *"But you must continue in the things which you have learned and been assured of, knowing from whom you have learned them"* (2 Timothy 3:14).

Regardless of your condition, the best medical prescription in the world is of no value if you don't take it. When the Lord shows you a path of victorious living, you stay on that road. That's why a post-checkup visit is not only helpful – it is essential.

Here are the questions you need to answer:

☐ Name a negative stronghold you would like to remove from your mind.

☐ Can you identify a behavior that is the result of wrong thinking?

☐ What bad habit would you like to eliminate? What will take it's place?

☐ If you had to name one excuse you use for failure, what would it be?

☐ What is your greatest fear? How do you plan to overcome it?

☐ List the two greatest thoughts that seem to dominate your thought life. Are they help or a hindrance?

☐ How does faulty thinking produce wrong beliefs.

☐ If you had to describe your core beliefs, what would they be?

☐ How does doubt hinder miracles?

☐ How many days of repetition does it usually take for a habit to form?

☐ Name a lie of Satan he would like you to believe as truth.

☐ Identify something that entered your mind and found its way to your heart.

☐ What is a harmful mind-pattern and how can it affect your life?

☐ Name a surprising result you have received by asking for the Lord helps.

☐ What are the best ways to meditate on God's Word?

☐ Has the devil ever made you feel like a failure? How did it affect your behavior?

☐ What is meant by "corrupt communication?"

☐ What is your best method of proclaiming the message of Christ?

- [ ] How do you filter what comes into your hearing?

- [ ] What is the primary source of your faith and belief?

- [ ] What steps do you take to make certain your will lines up with God's will?

- [ ] Name a "want to" you have changed to a "will to."

- [ ] Why is change the product of human effort sustained by divine help?

- [ ] Why is it true that you alone are in control of your will?

- [ ] What steps do you take to help make God's thoughts your thoughts?

- [ ] How does the pain/pleasure principle affect your life?

- [ ] What are three ways we learn to avoid pain?

- [ ] How do our emotions affect our decisions?

- [ ] Name a time that discord or controversy robbed you of God's blessing. What did you do to resolve the matter?

- [ ] How does the name of Jesus give you power of attorney.

- [ ] Have you ever used the Word to cause Satan to flee? What happened?

- [ ] Describe the covenant relationship you have established with the Almighty.

Don't take these questions lightly. God examines our lives for a purpose and I believe He is in the process of doing something awesome in your life.

I pray you will allow His Word and His will to wash over you – not just from the neck up, but every part of your life. Experience His showers of blessing!

OTHER TITLES BY
DALE CARNEGIE BRONNER:

PASS THE BATON!

GUARD YOUR GATES!

HOME REMEDIES

THE ART OF WAITING

PLANNING YOUR SUCCESSION

FOR A COMPLETE LIST OF BOOKS AND RESOURCES
BY DR. DALE C. BRONNER

CONTACT:

WORD OF FAITH FAMILY WORSHIP CATHEDRAL
212 RIVERSIDE PARKWAY
AUSTELL, GA 30168
PHONE 770-874-8400

www.dalebronner.com